TUMBLING TECHNIQUES
ILLUSTRATED

TED BURNS teaches at Herbert Hoover High School, San Diego, and has coached wrestling, track, basketball, and boys' and girls' tumbling.

TUMBLING TECHNIQUES
ILLUSTRATED

By

TED BURNS

Designed and Illustrated by

TYLER MICOLEAU

THE RONALD PRESS COMPANY • NEW YORK

TABLE OF CONTENTS

ACKNOWLEDGMENTS

The author wishes to express his gratitude to the following: Stanley M. Rose, former member of the U. S. C. Gymnastic Team, who assisted in the preparation of a glossary of known tumbling stunts and in selecting those most appropriate for presentation, criticized and corrected illustrations of complex movements, and demonstrated personally the twisting somersaults on the lawn of the National City (California) Recreation Center, where he was employed as supervisor; Professor Fred Kasch, Chairman of the Physical Education Department, San Diego State College, for demonstration coaching of the author's advanced pupils and and for being readily available for consultation throughout the preparation of this manuscript; Coach Charlie Pond, University of Illinois, for his extended loan of 16 m.m. films showing Dickie Browning's outstanding techniques; Ben Price, veteran Los Angeles judge of tumbling and trampoline events, for his patient explanation of form from a judge's point of view; Mrs. M. Thoornebrook, of the San Diego dance studios bearing her name, for demonstrations of coaching young pupils who are at present headline professional acrobats, dancers, and skaters; Jack Blake, Assistant Director of the Audio-visual Department, San Diego City Schools, for procuring all the available professionally made motion pictures of tumbling and for providing facilities for the enlargement of individual frames; and the Public Relations Department, University of California at Los Angeles, for permission to make 16 m.m. motion pictures of the 1955 National Intercollegiate Gymnastic Meet.

Chapter 1
INTRODUCTION TO TUMBLING

TUMBLING IS FUN. To fly through the air unencumbered by assisting apparatus is one of the most thrilling of human experiences. When landings are *with the greatest of ease,* the sensation is one of exquisite pleasure. And few spectacular thrills are greater than the vicarious experience of apparently death-defying routines, which are actually neither difficult nor dangerous.

Among young people of junior high school age and upward, the popularity of tumbling is limited only by available facilities. Whoever hesitates to agree that *every American kid is entitled to a tumbling experience* needs only to observe a random group of teen-agers at free tumbling practice. They love it! And so do their audiences.

THE PLAN OF THE BOOK. The author's purpose is to explain what the tumbler does in order to make his body do something. That *something to do* (the tumbler's technique) as related to *what happens as a result* is what the young tumbler needs to know. There is a difference.

TUMBLING IS PROBABLY THE BEST PHYSICAL DEVELOPMENT EXERCISE. Tumbling builds the right amount of muscle for efficient body control and simultaneously develops acute co-ordination. The tumbler has the built-in reflexes for effective action in any athletic activity—individual or team game. Men and women tumblers tend to conform to masculine and feminine physical ideals. Tumbling also develops stamina (toughness plus endurance) which, combined with balance and agility, insures against accidents in even the roughest sports.

TUMBLING IS DELIGHTFUL COMMUNITY ENTERTAINMENT. If the objectives of one's community organization are character-building and educational, a tumbling team will win public favor and support while the participant enjoys the supreme thrills of audience response.

TUMBLING IS FOR EVERYONE. Training accounts for much greater differences in ability than inheritance does. In tumbling, not all the fast learners go the furthest. A slow start should be nothing but a challenge.

TUMBLING IS A STRENUOUS AND DRAMATIC COMPETITIVE SPORT. In many high schools and colleges, students may elect gymnastics as a minor sport. Packed auditoriums and enthusiastic audience responses at meets indicate that, properly publicized, gymnastic contests will draw capacity crowds.

TUMBLING IS SAFE, if you don't horse. Another person upside down several feet over a mat is no joking matter. Don't try to be funny at first. The comedy act comes later; it's not for beginners.

Work from the mat up rather than from the aerial down. The stunts on or just over the mat will give the development and skill to avoid injury as you spring higher and turn faster.

Checks of pure physical ability are suggested for the first dangerous stunt in techniques to follow; note these carefully and don't try something you can't possibly accomplish. Don't do the high flips alone, any more than, as a novice, you would go swimming alone.

EQUIPMENT AND ATTIRE. Mats are, for most of us, where and as we find them. The popularity of tumbling is increasing, and more and better mats are becoming available to most of us. Numerous short mats can be fitted together for the routines. A wet towel under the edges where they join will prevent much slipping. In addition, they should be tied together before an exhibition. A cover will help also.

When you make the team and enter a meet, you'll have to wear a prescribed uniform. For practice, the lightest and freest clothing you can wear is best. For boys, trunks and supporter are adequate. For girls, a play suit or shorts and a light sweater are fine. If you wear a leotard, watch out for the zipper in the back on the rolls; you'll have to pad it. Men and women usually need light shoes, but teen-agers usually prefer to go barefooted. Basketball shoes or their equivalents won't be very comfortable or efficient, because you need to feel that you're gripping the mat with your toes.

Stage costumes may be in character. An artistic act featuring the performers for their skill or standing may emphasize each performer's physique or figure as well as skill.

TUMBLING IS THE CREATION AND CONTROL OF MOMENTUM. A routine is the performance of series of stunts which flow into each other, preceding stunts affecting the form and nature of those which follow. It is of the utmost importance to make each unit in a series affect the unit to follow it in some way—to make it easier, speed it up, increase its height, change direction, or slow up or finish. Beginning with your first practice period, work to *feel* the effect of one stunt upon the one to follow, and to make the transition between the two so smooth that you don't sense it and that your audience doesn't perceive it as a transition.

Chapter 2
FROM FORWARD ROLL TO
DOUBLE FORWARD SOMERSAULT

It is usual and logical to begin a tumbling experience by practicing forward rolls. The forward roll is the easiest stunt to learn and leads directly to dives, which may be sensational in a novice meet or act. Long or high dives lead easily and naturally to the forward somersault, generally regarded as a headline essential in the repertoire of the advanced tumbler.

The primary concept to master is that of the body as a dynamic, neuromuscular machine. If you squat, duck, and fall forward, you may, in some awkward manner, come up on your feet facing forward. But don't count on even that as a certainty. To tumble gracefully, you must deliberately create and control the force, type, and direction of momentum.

Forward momentum is created by a run, a spring from the balls of the feet, or both. For a forward roll, only a slight spring is necessary, but it must be deliberate and calculated with regard to direction and force.

Another type of momentum is circular. The tumbler must convert forward to circular momentum at will. He must also be able to create circular momentum independently of movement forward, backward, up, or down. The tuck is one basic means of converting to or creating circular momentum.

In the forward roll it is necessary to *create* circular momentum by means of the tuck.

The body is not simply curled so that it *may* roll. The movement into the tuck, as illustrated, will *make* the body roll. And the more vigorous the tuck, the greater the circular momentum and the faster the roll.

9

In the forward roll, both forward and circular momentum is moderate. In the dive, the tuck converts rapid forward and downward momentum to circular for a comfortable landing. In the forward somersault, circular momentum is created by a tuck while the body is still rising. This turns the body over in time for a safe landing.

The "flip" of the forward somersault should be visualized in the tuck of the forward roll. The difference is only that of the greater violence of the tuck for a "flip."

The dynamic control of the tuck in the roll must precede mastery of the flip. You must master the technique of the tuck, not simply in order to do forward rolls, but to be able to execute the flip of the forward somersault later on.

In both the dive and the forward somersault you must create forward momentum in order to achieve a maximum of upward momentum. A simple jump upward creates only negligible momentum, but rapid forward speed may be converted to spectacular height if you know how.

A fast, low-hopping baseball ricochets upward upon encountering the side slope of a rise of ground. The body, as a dynamic machine, may ricochet at will by means of a bounce take-off. The direction of the bounce is controlled by the angle of forward lean, provided the line of force of the combined leg drive and upward arm swing coincides with the forward-lean angle. (Note the forward-lean take-off of the dive, as illustrated.)

You must understand and remember that a bounce landing intended to set you up for a spring upward may *absorb* shock and thus *kill* momentum. You may find yourself jumping high preceding the upward spring and simply using the leg muscles to ease the shock of landing. The spring, then, becomes little better than a dead-lift jump. In order to carry out the ricochet design, the speed and force of the leg drive, or stamp, of the spring must match the speed of the forward movement. There is not time for a spring from a low squat. The muscular reaction of the "bounce" must be of great speed and must stiffen the leg muscles as they drive upward in opposition to the forward momentum, which they must direct upward. Much as the ricocheting baseball encounters a solid sloping wall, the tumbler ricochets as his forward movement encounters an upward line of force (resulting from his take-off spring) which will not "give."

Forward momentum may be checked by a second upward spring, as at the finish of a dive. Opening into a full arch checks circular momentum.

In the forward roll, circular momentum is created by means of a tuck and is checked by the rise to erect stance. In the dive, downward momentum is converted to circular by means of a tuck and may be reconverted upward by a high bounce, which serves both to keep the body within bounds and to constitute a spectacular finish. In the forward somersault, circular momentum is created by the tuck in the air, then checked by the body opening which prepares for the landing.

A one-and-a-half (a forward somersault in which circular momentum is permitted to continue for an additional half turn in the air and to proceed to complete the second turn on the mat) is possible should a tumbler of superlative ability choose to perfect the tricky timing which would be necessary. The double forward somersault is the tumbler's stunt par excellence, and it is only rarely accomplished by either amateurs or professionals.

11

THE FORWARD ROLL

Face forward. Point your toes straight ahead, feet slightly apart; otherwise, stand at attention.

Raise your arms and lean forward, shifting your weight to the balls of your feet.

Reach for the mat and squat. Hands shoulder-width apart, aim about an arm's length in front of your toes. Squat to approximately a 90° angle.

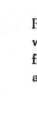

Upon solid hand contact, fingers spread for maximum control, extend your knees by a moderate spring, evenly from the toes of both feet. At the same time, duck your head under your arms, thrusting your forehead toward the knees. Bend your elbows, resisting slightly in order to effect a controlled landing on the back of your neck and shoulders.

Curl your backbone to bring your thighs against your chest. Simultaneously, bend your knees past a 90° angle.

Convert forward to circular momentum by flexing your body into a tight ball and roll freely.

Reach hard for your shins. Begin a bent-arm forward and upward arm swing the instant the roll carries your weight past your shoulders.

Grasp your shins and pull. Reach and grab forcefully to speed up your roll. Draw your feet to the mat close to your hips.

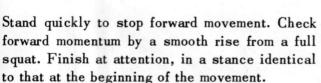

Release your shins as a forward-lean, squat balance is assured. Reach out to continue forward movement at a smooth pace and to prevent falling backward.

Stand quickly to stop forward movement. Check forward momentum by a smooth rise from a full squat. Finish at attention, in a stance identical to that at the beginning of the movement.

(The forward roll should be fast enough to make the smooth but abrupt rise necessary in order to check it. The raise, thus, is not a dead-lift extension from a squat, but a live, controlled movement.)

THE DIVE

Sprint for a fast take-off.

Land with feet even, arms back. Shorten the final stride and draw your feet in line for a power spring forward and upward from both feet. (Practice to control the height gained from your final stride so as to preserve a maximum of forward speed.)

Take off from a forward-lean crouch. Keep your back straight for the landing and take-off. Perfect the 45° forward-lean angle for greatest possible length of dive.

Drive for a straight-line, full-body extension. Synchronize your arm-swing and leg-drive for simultaneous completion. Stretch out, legs together and toes pointed.

Project yourself at a 45° angle. Hold the straight-line extension until your chest clears the height intended.

14

Arch from the hips to throw your legs upward, forcing your body into a long stretch parallel to the mat. Keep your legs tightly together, knees straight and toes pointed.

Bend at your hips as you pass the peak of your dive. Reach for the mat and duck your head under. Keep your knees straight as long as practicable; keep your toes pointed all the way through the stunt.

Land on both shoulders and the back of your neck. Use your hand contact and arm support to guide you into a fast but smooth landing.

Tuck fast and grasp the shins hard to keep the speedy landing under control.

Make a snappy, bounce finish. Convert circular momentum to height by a flashy, high spring. This adds class and excitement to an already spectacular movement. Furthermore, there is little else you can do to check the terrific forward momentum.

THE FORWARD SOMERSAULT

Spring from your toes as for a dive. Take off from a nearly vertical forward lean, because your objective is maximum height rather than distance. Take off at full speed; don't hesitate for a deliberate "pounce."

Chop down hard. Begin the knee-lift the instant your feet leave the mat, and bring your shins into the hand-clasp as fast as possible. Create maximum circular momentum by means of the downward lunge of the head and shoulders as well as the arm-swing and grab.

Tuck fast and hard. Make the downward lunge and leg-slap turn you over. Pull hard against your legs at the instant of contact in order to force the turn to the full 360°. Aim to reach the vertical, upside-down position at the point of maximum height.

(Do the forward somersault simply as a very fast roll, *over* instead of *on* the mat. Execute the tucked roll—as for a long, high dive—before rather than after you land.)

Tuck tight for a fast turn. You are free to generate circular momentum by a violent tuck action, independently of upward movement, while your body is rising. The tighter your tuck, the faster you'll turn.

Keep the turn true and free. Avoid any conflicting tension which may cause a twist or wobble. Keep your legs together and your toes pointed. Simply *permit* circular momentum to bring you into the three-quarter turn position. At this point, relax the hands and begin to look upward.

Drive the feet downward. Get your legs under your body. Put your feet where you want them to be; don't depend upon a relaxed fall to drop you into a graceful landing. Look straight ahead from a straight back as you fall.

Open as wide as your height over the mat will permit. The full extension and arch, as illustrated, represents an ideal. Stop circular momentum by as wide an extension as you can manage. Land on the balls of your feet, knees bent slightly to cushion the shock. (You may extend sharply in an instantaneous spring upward for a bounce finish, or to carry momentum over into a succeeding stunt.)

17

ONE AND ONE-HALF FORWARD SOMERSAULT

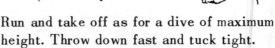

Run and take off as for a dive of maximum height. Throw down fast and tuck tight.

Hold your tuck through the position from which you normally open.

Kick out of your tuck in reverse (head down and feet up) and you face the mat.

Use your hands and arms to guide your body into a second tuck.

Steer into a true, straight-ahead roll without diminishing speed. Spring for height or into a forward somersault as your roll is completed.

(Try this first into very soft shavings in an oversize pit, later into deep sand. Don't attempt this stunt on an ordinary mat until your timing is perfect and 100 per cent predictable. This somersault into a dive, followed by a somersault and subsequently a dive and roll, should be very impressive.)

THE DOUBLE FORWARD SOMERSAULT

Slam your thighs against your chest. Throw down for your tuck while you are still going up. Make your take-off and your knee raise one continuous, very fast movement.

Tuck very tight as well as very fast, forehead between the insides of your knees. Pull your shins in to force your heels in close to your buttocks. Keep your knees far enough apart to permit your forehead to rest between them in order to avoid possible head injury upon landing. Force the insides of your knees tightly against your head.

You will not have time to kick out of your tuck into a landing; a low squat is good enough. Raise your head, throw your arms forward for balance, and grip with your feet as you strike the mat.

THE FORWARD TUCK

LESSON PLANS

Step I

Master a single forward roll as a graceful, dynamic movement. The technique principally involved is the creation and control of circular momentum.

Step II

Make the transition from forward rolls to dives by gradually springing harder from a standing broad-jump position. Continue until standing dives of maximum length are automatically in good form. Try to clear a length equivalent to your own height, as an intermediate goal. The initial technique involved in this step is the creation of forward momentum by means of a leg drive. The trick is speeded up, and emphasizes control rather than power, as the tuck converts forward to circular momentum.

Step III

Shorten each dive to about a two-thirds maximum effort and proceed directly into another. The transition should be so smooth that you feel no sensation of ending one dive and beginning another. To a spectator, the two dives should appear as one continuous movement. Practice until the two dives seem, both to you and your spectators, as one stunt.

Next, achieve the same smooth, rhythmic progression in a series of forward rolls. Proceeding again to dives, do a series of varying lengths and at varying speeds, making each dive of a series of the same length and speed. Finally, alternate rolls and dives. This is, in effect, rolling into a dive two to four times in a continuous series. The technique involved in Step III is that of control of transitions from forward to circular and back to forward momentum. The concept of rhythmic progressions from one stunt to another through an exhibition or competitive routine is vital to an artistic performance. A routine of moderate difficulty that is beautifully executed is of greater value than a series of very difficult stunts merely accomplished. *Finesse* in performance should be a matter of concern at this stage, and, assuming mastery of form, *finesse* depends upon rhythm.

Step IV

Gradually increase the speed of your run, preceding a dive take-off. Accomplish the ricochet effect by a fast take-off. Vary the comparative heights and lengths of dives at this stage. You may dive over four to ten partners, kneeling close together; then progress to three-wide and, later, four-wide, two-high pyramids. Diving through the legs of one or more partners in the headstand position is an amusing and pleasant variation. Finish the long and high dives with a high bounce as illustrated.

Step V

Dive for a complete lay-out, body fully extended and parallel to the mat. Perfect a 45° forward-lean take-off. Maximum height should be reached midway through the dive. Work up to a clearance of shoulder height and double that distance. Men and teen-age boys should achieve greater than head height through practicing diving as an exercise. During this stage, do at least twenty maximum effort dives three times a week.

Step VI

Work on a forward somersault until you can land with your knees only slightly bent. This is rather a large order stated in a very simple sentence, but the front somersault is neither very difficult to learn nor to do—once it is learned.

There are two hazards which must be overcome: physical and psychological.

When *can* you do a front somersault, once your "thinking-felling" apparatus will *permit* you to do it? You'll want a safe *physical* margin. When you can dive over an obstacle of shoulder height you'll have from 0.5 to 0.6 of a second between take-off and landing. If you can clear your own height on a dive, you'll have more time and room for a tucked flip than you actually need.

Tumbling ability involves both what you know and what you are. What you know will never compensate for what you are not. Let's assume that you understand fairly well everything explained in this chapter. If you *are* a neuromuscular machine which can, with moderate ease, dive over something of shoulder height, you may be sure that you *can* get all the way over on a front somersault—provided your feelings about the matter do not interfere.

Your feelings! If you didn't have any—about this particular matter—you could do the flip. But then you wouldn't want to, and there'd be no thrill if or when you did. But you do have feelings, and whatever part of you it is that these feelings represent must be convinced. This is the psychological hazard. You'll have to go slowly and be very thorough.

A simple beginning is advised to convince yourself gradually that somersaults are safe and fun. Rolling and then somersaulting over a rolled mat has been widely practiced by large heterogeneous groups, including armed service units. Roll over the mat first; then, spring harder and bounce off of it, striking your shoulders; later, spring still higher and land sitting on it; finally, clear it, landing in a low squat. Continue until you feel safe without the mat, after which you'll never need it again.

The question I have heard hundreds of times: "How long will it take?" To get this far, I don't know. It depends partly upon what you are now—your sex, age, physical condition, previous athletic experience, natural athletic ability. Also upon the regu-larity of a training program. An organized class or club will help a great deal. If you're 10 and a boy, or 30 and a man, it may take 2 years, but it would be well worth it. If you're a teen-ager, that is, an average boy or an athletic girl, 6 months should do it. If you're over 30, have fun but don't hold your breath until you win a medal. Within these probable outcomes, it's up to you. *Almost* anything *can* happen.

Somersaults from a low board over water will help a lot. A bad landing will sting, but think nothing of it. Do a once-over and go in feet first. When this much is in good form, spring high and turn fast for a one-and-a-half.

Don't proceed from the pool to the mat, or you'll be sorry. From a mat workout to a diving board workout is fine. The same goes for the trampoline: get a good workout on the mat, then a trampoline workout to stabilize your flips. But don't confuse the take-offs. A high bounce take-off (as for the low board take-off) will get you practically nowhere on a mat. Neither will a fast bounce take-off from a low board or a trampoline. You can readily learn different take-off techniques appropriate for each of these three surfaces, provided you understand and perfect the very different reflexes involved. After the take-off, techniques are similar and all workouts should affect very favorably both what you are and what you know you can do.

The spot for a forward somersault is a hand back of the neck. The spotter provides whatever circular momentum seems lacking for a complete turn.

Chapter 3
FROM BACKWARD ROLL TO
DOUBLE BACKWARD SOMERSAULT

The backward roll reverses the action of the forward roll. The arms are jerked upward and the head and shoulders thrown backwards while a a powerful knee lift slaps the thighs against the chest and pulls the shins into the upraised hands. The speed of the knee lift determines the power of circular momentum, and the tightness of the tuck controls the speed at which the body turns.

The backward somersault is the "spin" of the backward roll *over* instead of on the mat. The throw backwards proceeds further, and circular momentum built up by the knee lift accentuates the spin because the mat no longer interferes.

Backward somersaults may be done as *spotters* (from a stationary squat), in series (*whipbacks*), or—most frequently—in routines, after a series of flipflaps or a roundoff-flipflap.

A *gainer* is executed by means of several running steps forward, a hop on the left foot, and a vigorous kick upward with the right leg simultaneously with a trunk, head, and arm throw backward. Gainers may be in tuck or layout position as the left leg is drawn into alignment with the right leg. The layout position, obviously, requires the greater height and is possible only in a highly skillful performance.

The *kickback,* usually a girl's stunt, is similar but is fast and free; a precise tuck or layout is not attempted, and great height is not necessary.

The double backward somersault is outranked in difficulty only by the double forward somersault. Sensationally surprising a few years ago, it is now expected as one routine climax in a collegiate or senior A. A. U. championship performance. The tumbler must lift his center of gravity approximately to his own height in order to gain time for the double rotation. The knee lift is so fast that it makes the take-off seem a "slap" against the mat and brings the knees into the hands before maximum height is reached. The second turn is a continuation of the spin and results from holding the tuck through the second revolution. An extremely expert performer may manage a fairly extended landing and a take-off into a subsequent trick.

THE BACKWARD ROLL

Stand at attention. with your back to the mat.

Sit with a slight backward lean.

While learning, place your hands at your hips to cushion your landing and assist your backward roll with a push. Later, extend your arms forward at this stage.

Curve your back forward, roll backward, and pull your knees to your chest with sufficient vigor to generate the backward momentum you need.

Hold a tight tuck and permit momentum to carry you through the roll.

THE BACKWARD ROLL

Shift your hands to the mat back of your neck as the back of your head contacts the mat.

Hold your tuck as your hips roll back of your shoulders.

Push up to relieve your head from the weight of your body as you roll directly over to your forehead.

Push away from the mat as your forehead clears. Push with sufficient force to bring you up on to your feet, if this is your final roll of a series or a single roll.

Stand erect, at attention, to finish a series or a single roll.

THE BACKWARD SOMERSAULT

Check your balance for a standing somersault.

Swing your arms backward for a violent throw upward as you sink to approximately 90° hip-and-knee angle, on your toes.

Take off from your toes on a leg drive straight upward. Throw your arms, head, and shoulders backward with the final push from your toes.

Lift your legs into your arms as a follow-through of your take-off drive.

Pull hard against your shins to tighten your tuck as your turn.

Hold your tight tuck through your upside-down position.

Release your hand grip as you go
into your three-quarter turn. Look
up as you release your shins.

Kick out of your tuck and raise your
arms upon your release. Make your
kick-out a vigorous movement, in
keeping with the speed of your tuck.

Draw your legs under your
hips and raise your arms for
as erect a landing as your
skill at a given time will
permit.

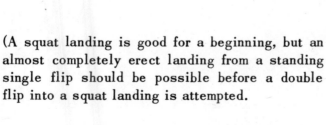

(A squat landing is good for a beginning, but an
almost completely erect landing from a standing
single flip should be possible before a double
flip into a squat landing is attempted.

GAINER

Run fast and spring into a vertical take-off. Kick for maximum height and upward momentum.

Throw your head and shoulders backward and pull both legs into your arms for a tight tuck.

Execute the backward turn as for any backward somersault in tuck position.

Open at a three-quarter turn and drive your legs under you.

Land as nearly erect as possible, using your arms to balance.

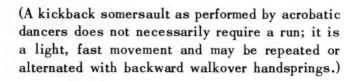

(A kickback somersault as performed by acrobatic dancers does not necessarily require a run; it is a light, fast movement and may be repeated or alternated with backward walkover handsprings.)

THE DOUBLE BACKWARD
SOMERSAULT

Throw and spring straight upward. Drive your feet against the mat, knees only slightly bent, for the fastest possible take-off. Slap your thighs into your chest instantly, following your leg extension. The power of your knee raise, bringing your shins into your hand grip while your body is still rising, will convert to speed of circular momentum as your tuck is completed.

Draw into a very tight tuck for the fastest possible circular movement.

Hold your tuck past your second head-down position.

Release your grip as your head comes up toward your take-off on your second revolution.

Lean forward and reach out to check circular movement upon landing. Try to hold your balance preliminary to standing erect.

Perfect a build-up routine which will develop the speed and force necessary to enable you to raise your center of gravity to an altitude greater than your own height.)

THE BACKWARD TUCK

LESSON PLANS

Step I

Perfect a single, conventional backward roll.

Step II

Develop control of a series of three to eight backward rolls.

Step III

Perfect a single backward roll in the manner of the forward roll, hands free rather than against the mat; grasp your shins with your hands as you bring your thighs to your chest with such violence as to motivate the roll without a hand-and-arm push against the mat.

Step IV

Check your ability to spring high enough and flex your legs fast enough to do an unassisted backward somersault. Can you do a standing high jump over a bar or other mark at waist height? If you *can*, and hold your balance, you *are* what it is necessary to *be* in order to do a tucked backward somersault. If you're not, support by a belt while you try takes on the nature of a not-too-funny joke. You can't reason yourself into leg muscles which will lift your center of gravity approximately four-sevenths of your height. Make standing high jumps an exercise, beginning with whatever height you can clear comfortably twenty times in a few minutes. The knee raise is as important as the spring; slap your thighs against your chest on every jump. Continue until you can do a standing high jump repeatedly and easily well over waist height.

Step V

Accept an assist from one partner sitting and another spotting to lift and turn you by placing a hand just below the small of your back. When you can land repeatedly with your knees extended at least 90°, repeat with a steadily diminishing assist from a partner in prone position.

Step VI

Practice unassisted back somersaults until you gain complete confidence; then the stunt is easy to do.

The spot for the backward somersault is a flat palm, fingers spread, just below the small of the back. The spotter may provide lift or circular momentum as needed by the twist of the wrist.

Chapter 4
FROM SHOULDER
SPRING TO PIKE FULL

Springs from the neck and shoulders from a forward roll or dive are, technically, neck springs. Similar springs from a prone position or an interrupted backward roll are generally called kips.

Head and neck springs are flashy stunts for novice performances. They may be effectively incorporated into novice routines—in a series, to begin or finish a routine, or between other stunts. Variations, such as a boy's high, arched spring over a girl partner in a back bend or a kneeling position, may climax an act.

Both springs should be light and free and appear easy to do. Mastery of these stunts in the form illustrated is, however, very strenuous exercise. The lightness and freedom desired comes only after the development of a physique capable of advanced stunts, and prolonged practice of head and neck springs may play a vital part in the building of such a physique.

The leg swing of the head spring, neck spring, or kip is also that of the difficult and advanced pike full. Greater height is required for a layout because the extended body turns more slowly than the ball created by a tuck. But the turn of the layout is slow only by comparison; it must actually be too fast to follow easily with the eye, and the principal movement which creates this almost incredible circular momentum is that of the leg swing.

The pike full is, thus, substantially a head spring high over the mat. If you can spring high enough to dive over a bar placed at head height you have the first requirement. If you can do a series of high, arched head springs, knees straight during the leg swing and almost straight for each landing, you have the second. When you can do both you *are* what it is necessary to *be* in order to do a forward somersault which achieves a layout through part of the 360° revolution. If you use head and neck springs as development exercise to build a physique which can exert a leg swing powerful enough to propel the body through the air to an erect landing from a head spring or kip, the same swing will turn you through the arc of a bounder full or a pike full after the high point of your spring in either stunt.

Forward somersaults in series with the body extended into a layout at some stage and a semi-layout during most of each revolution are called *bounder fulls*. The pike full is precisely as a pike front somersault into water, excepting that you kick out for a tumbler's landing.

31

FROG-STYLE PRESS
TO HEAD BALANCE

Hold a controlled squat hand balance. Place the heels of your hands on the mat, shoulder-width apart. Flatten your palms but keep your fingers slightly arched and straight forward. Rest the inside of your thighs, just above your knees, on your arms just above your elbows. Tip forward until your legs approximately parallel the mat.

Place your head, just above the hairline, as far from each hand as the hands are apart. Hold a squat head and hand balance.

Draw your hips to a direct, stable balance above the tripod formed by your head and hands; then press straight up.

Arch so as to place your hips above your shoulders and your ankles above head. Lock your entire arch, knees stiff and toes pointed.

SPRING-OVER AND TWIST
(an exercise)

Assume a front bridge position.

Spring over to a high arch.

Twist. Lift your free leg high and walk over. To twist to the right, thrust your right shoulder backwards and whip your left arm across your chest. Reverse arm and shoulder action for a left turn.

Return to your front bridge, opposite but otherwise identical to your starting position.

This exercise strengthens and toughens your most vulnerable joints, limbers your back, and establishes the arch and twist reflexes. Do the entire exercise at least ten times twisting to your left and ten times twisting to your right. If you lose your balance, start over; it's the ten straight that counts. (Everyone use hand assist at first. Boys, when you're tough enough, touch head and toes only.)

Balance for another spring.

THE HEADSPRING

Take off from both feet. Spring from your toes, feet even and close together, into an easy dive, straight ahead.

Dive onto your hands. Keep your fingers spread and pointed straight ahead.

Use your arm and shoulder muscles to effect an easy landing on the head, at the hairline. Permit the legs to lag naturally during the dive and landing.

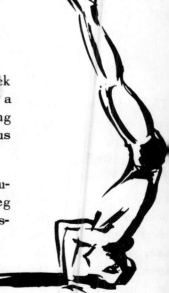

Swing hard from your hips. Pull with your back and buttock muscles to swing your legs in a wide arc, from toes actually or nearly touching the mat into a strong body arch, in one continuous movement.

Push hard with your hands and forehead continuously during the leg swing. Combine your leg swing and arm push to exert the strongest possible pressure against the mat.

Swing for range and speed. The wider the angle of the leg swing and the faster the swing is accomplished, the greater the pressure against the mat. Swing your feet as far and as fast as possible, knees straight and toes pointed throughout.

Arch into a 45° take-off. As your feet, hips, and shoulders pass a vertical reverse-balance, launch yourself into the air by means of a snap arch and a final snap push. Continue your arm push after your head leaves the mat and until circular momentum pulls your hands off the mat.

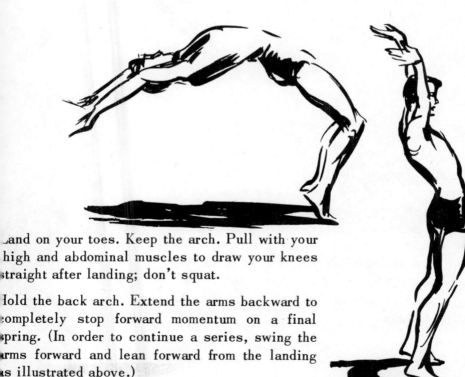

Land on your toes. Keep the arch. Pull with your thigh and abdominal muscles to draw your knees straight after landing; don't squat.

Hold the back arch. Extend the arms backward to completely stop forward momentum on a final spring. (In order to continue a series, swing the arms forward and lean forward from the landing as illustrated above.)

THE KIP

Touch your toes to the mat back of your head.

Snap push to clear the mat. Follow through from the final push off the mat into a forward arm swing.

Swing into an upward body extension. Keep your legs straight, together, and your toes pointed throughout the leg swing. Make your leg swing as fast as possible and aim through a high shoulder balance into a back arch.

Arch high and fast. Force your leg swing to carry you past the vertical shoulder balance position. Bend your knees only enough to continue the the curved line of your back arch. Push with your hands throughout your leg swing.

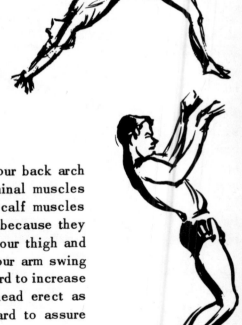

As you land on your toes, stiffen your back arch and pull with your thigh and abdominal muscles to avoid going into a squat. Your calf muscles should push your toes into the mat because they serve as an anchor against which your thigh and torso muscles may pull. Combine your arm swing with a head and shoulder lunge forward to increase upper-body momentum. Hold your head erect as you continue your arm swing forward to assure vertical balance.

PRESS-UP TO
A HAND BALANCE

PIKE-STYLE
PRESS-UP

(Achieve easy control of a pike press up to a head balance first.) Place your hands shoulder width apart, fingers spread and straight forward. Hold your head up.

Arms and knees straight, shift your center of gravity forward until all of your weight rests on your hands.

Keep your back straight while you exert finger, arm, and shoulder muscles to the utmost to form a brace against which the hip extensors may pull for the straight-knee, toes-pointed leg raise.

Rest your legs across your upper arms as for a frog-style headstand.

Draw your hips forward, back straight, and press your legs upward.

Reach for the ceiling with your feet, pressing upward from your finger tips to sharply pointed toes, tensing all of the intervening muscles in your upward reach.

(Bend at the elbows only as necessary to maintain balance as you swing into a body arch, your feet above your head. If you tend to fall backward, press with the heels of your hands; if forward, with your fingers as you raise your head. Press upward throughout the length of your body for a controlled balance and a moderate arch.)

BOUNDER FULL

Take off as for a high dive. Build up forward momentum by sprinting whatever distance available space will permit. Convert forward to upward momentum by the ricochet effect of your upward take-off.

Bend forward to permit your hips to reach maximum height at the high point of the spring.

Begin the leg swing precisely as illustrated for a head spring.

Create "pinwheel" circular momentum around your hips as a pivotal point.

Do this by means of a head-and-shoulder lunge downward, back straight, and a leg swing upward, knees straight and toes pointed.

Speed up your leg swing to carry into an upside-down body extension as your center of gravity reaches its highest point.
(Visualize this position as precisely similar to its counterpart in the headspring, as immediately preceding the snap arch which accentuates the spin.)

°Carry your leg swing into a back arch. Manipulate your arms chiefly for balance at this point. Permit circular momentum to carry you almost into a horizontal position before breaking your arch. Keep your back straight throughout the turn.

Swing the arms upward and bend slightly at the waist and knees.

Carry the arm swing well forward and follow through with the leg swing to get your feet under your hips.

Draw your body into an arch preceding your landing. Throw the arms upward and back to stop circular momentum on a single full or as the final stunt of a routine. Land with your arms in front of your body if you wish to take off for a succeeding stunt.

39

THE PIKE SEQUENCE

LESSON PLANS

Step I

First, can you get into the extreme position preceding a full kip? Try this. Make it an exercise project until you can do it easily. Touch your toes back of your head and return to the relaxed prone position. Make each leg swing and return deliberate: maintain body alignment; avoid any jerk, wobble, twist, or knee or ankle bend. You need control and rhythm at this stage, not speed.

The spring-over and twist exercise will be possible, if not graceful or comfortable for most, right away. This helps to develop the arch and limbers the back preparatory to more advanced stunts.

Also, at this stage develop control of your body as you extend into an upside-down balance. Don't stay upside down too long at a stretch; do five of these deliberate press-ups, then another exercise or stunt, then five more headstands, until you've done 15 to 20 each exercise period.

Step II

Practicing head springs, then neck springs, from folded or rolled layers of mats is the simplest and most effective approach to springs from a flat surface. Few beginners can make even fair landings from a level mat surface. There is nothing very terrible about crash landings on the seat of your trunks (and it does amuse your audience), but this type of practice doesn't seem to lead to anything better. Try an easy spring from three layers of mat (rolled or folded). A partner should hold the mat steady if it is rolled. The height afforded will enable you to land on your feet and pull up to an erect position rather easily.

Continue but speed up the action. Landing on one's feet after a flying take-off from head and hands is a new and thrilling experience. You'll probably hook your knees and land in a low squat at first. Gradually decrease the knee angle during the take-off and progress to an extended (layout) landing.

Step III

When you get the feel of the head spring, try the neck spring. When safe, comfortable landings are the rule, gradually straighten the knees and make the leg swing generate momentum. You'll feel a new power, and you'll begin to land with your legs under you and only slightly bent.

Begin over—head springs, then neck springs, from two mats. Soon you'll feel the power of the leg swing literally projecting you on flying take-offs, and two mats will be too high. Begin over from one layer of raised mat and continue until excellent form in both stunts is the rule.

Step IV

Perfect a single, good head spring from a level surface. Also, develop power and control of the leg swing in the head-down position by practicing the pike-style press-up to a head stand. This press-up to a head stand is preparatory to the press-up to a hand stand, which is basic to hand balancing, hand-to-hand acrobatics, and much of the popular free exercise event.

Step V

Perfect the neck spring from a level surface. Roll into it as a forward roll.

Step VI

Perfect the kip from a level surface, legs straight and toes touching the mat back of your head.

Step VII

Perfect head springs and neck springs in rhythmic sequences. Do a series of each separately and also alternate the two stunts so smoothly that spectators cannot recognize beginnings or endings of individual springs.

Step VIII

Begin a transition from a tightly tucked, high front somersault to a pike full. Gradually straighten your knees (don't clasp the shins) until you achieve the full layout in the upside-down position. This is a violently strenuous movement; don't rush your progress or include too many repetitions until it feels easy to do. Above all, don't land with your knees stiff: a habitual spring into a dive from the pike full landing will avoid this.

41

Chapter 5

HANDSPRINGS, KICKOVER
AND KICKBACK SOMERSAULTS

A kick-up to a handstand establishes the balance essential to the scissors-action leg swing through the handstand and into the arched landing of ordinary hand spring. Some progress should be made towards handstands of at least a few seconds duration, before good hand springs are expected.

In the hand spring the leg swing of the head spring is repeated, excepting that the legs are swung separately. The result is a freer, faster movement. Both the initial swing with the free leg and the follow-up of the take-off leg tend to lift the body so that very little weight need rest on the hands. Thus the hand snap may be a free push-away because the body is overbalanced in the direction of the arch.

The Arabian handspring is an effective finish of any stunt involving a dive onto the hands, or it may lead into a forward somersault.

The frontover is a slow hand spring involving an accentuated back bend. The push-away is minimized and the pull-up, a recovery from the back-bend position, is emphasized. Momentum being only an incidental factor, the take-off may be from the feet even and together. On the landing, the follow-up foot may even drop back of the push-off foot for a backward progression. Frontovers are ordinarily girls' stunts.

A walkover results when the follow-up (take-off) leg does not catch up with the kickover leg. The free leg (at the take-off) lands, and the follow-up leg strikes ahead a short walking stride. A rhythmic, forward movement is natural. The stunt may feature either a limber back and a split through the reverse-balance position or speed to give the body so strong a lift that progression into a walkover (often called kickover) somersault is natural and easy.

One-hand walkovers are particularly effective in parades or field entertainments.

Backward walkover hand springs may be at slow or moderate rhythm and often feature a split during the leg swing. Kickback somersaults must be extremely fast and may be as gainers during forward motion of the body.

KICK UP TO A HANDSTAND

Balance your weight on your hands and your take-off foot. Spread your fingers wide. Crouch for an easy spring from the toes of your take-off foot and a free swing upward with the opposite leg, toes pointed. Synchronize your push-off and upward swing. Experiment to determine the correct force.

Straighten the take-off leg. Make your take-off leg extension a smooth follow-through of the spring.

Check the swing of your free leg as you feel the weight of this side of your body balance evenly over your corresponding hand support.

Draw your legs together to form an arch. Make your arch an even curve along your calves, thighs, hips, and shoulders. Extend both ankles, toes pointed.

Stabilize your balance by manipulating your arm push, hand pressure, and arch. If you tend to overcast, push up, stretch up, press hard with your fingers, and raise your head. If you tend to fall backwards, let down, accentuate your arch, and press with the heels of your hands. Hold in approximately an ankles-over-ears vertical alignment. Snap down or twist to recover your feet.

43

THE FORWARD HANDSPRING

Begin your run a convenient distance from the mat in order to build up forward momentum.

Skip and throw down for a firm hand placement, fingers forward and spread about 18 inches in front of the take-off foot, your head up.

Spring from the ball of your forward foot and swing your free leg from your hip, thigh, and knee almost straight. Speed the follow-up swing of your take-off leg so as to carry into a legs-spread Y above a vertical torso.

Push off from the mat as your double leg swing closes in a scissors effect. Arch high (draw your hips upward), your knees bent only enough to carry out the line of your body arch.

Swing your arms vigorously upward in order to achieve a shoulder lift as high as possible upon landing. Land with your knees only slightly bent.

Carry your arms high in order to check circular momentum for a balanced landing. (You are in position to throw into a quick tuck and take off into a forward somersault.)

THE ARABIAN HANDSPRING

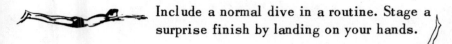

Include a normal dive in a routine. Stage a surprise finish by landing on your hands.

Use your hand contact to pin down this extreme of your body, causing your legs to swing in a fast arc over your head. Arch rapidly through the handstand position.

Push off vigorously and press your hips upward to maintain your arch. For the most spectacular gain of height and distance, push off as your leg swing reaches the 45° angle to the mat.

Land high, body extended. A strong arch with arms in swan position will check forward momentum for a controlled landing, or you may shift an arch to a forward lean, carrying your arms high and in front, and take off into a forward somersault.

(A dive into an Arabian handspring followed by a forward somersault constitutes a routine of moderate difficulty, and is likely to register as a surprise because it is not often done.)

THE WALKOVER
HANDSPRING

Take off as for an ordinary hand spring.

Swing your right leg as for the previously illustrated hand spring but exaggerate your arch.

Speed up your left leg swing, but not enough to catch up with your right leg.

Push off from the mat before your right foot lands.

Finish as having completed a normal walking stride, except for greater arch. Throw forward and repeat.

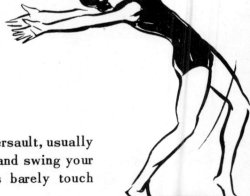

(Your approach to a walkover somersault, usually called a kickover, is to speed up and swing your legs higher until your fingertips barely touch through the handstand position.)

ONE-HAND WALKOVER

Throw down the arm corresponding to your take-off leg. Place your free arm across your chest or manipulate it for balance.

Whip your free leg over very fast to prevent your body from dropping toward your unsupported side.

Repeat in swingtime for a forward progression at approximately walking speed.

KICKOVER SOMERSAULT

Work to attain the speed and lift necessary to carry you straight over with only a light touch of the extended fingers of your contact hand to guide you.

Continue the light-touch one-hand hand spring technique, but with the speed and lift necessary to render any hand contact unnecessary.

(Repeat or alternate with one-hand walkover.)

THE BACK BEND

Stand flat-footed, heels 8 to 12 inches apart, toes out. While learning, place your feet for a broad, firm base. Bend your knees and raise your arms to confirm this substantial base.

Reach backward, arch your back, and slide your knees forward. Proceed deliberately to balance your hips over your heels as you increase your back bend.

Bend your knees while your back bend reaches your maximum range. Utilize an increasing knee bend in order to keep your hips over your heels as you reach down toward the mat.

Raise your hips high as your fingertips approach the mat. Keep your head back and watch the mat as you complete the bend.

Rock back to place your weight equally on your hands and feet.

Continue to press your hips upward as you increase your knee angle in order to assume a graceful arch.

RECOVERY FROM A BACK BEND

Push with your hands to bring your weight back over your feet.

Slide your hips forward. Bend your knees and shift your weight forward as your hands leave the mat.

Balance your hips over your heels as you begin the pull upward.

Keep your knees well forward in order to maintain this balance.

Press hard with your toes and pull hard with your thigh and abdominal muscles. Raise your arms toward your hips and knees in order to shift your body weight forward. Stand erect.

(This may be a long, hard pull while you're learning. The recovery is a development exercise for thigh and abdominal muscles as well as a test of a limber back. For best results, make it an exercise until the ability is established.

BACKWARD WALKOVER

(Strictly defined as an acrobatic dancing technique, walkovers involve continuous hand or foot contact with the mat. As illustrated, this and the preceding stunt are adaptations suitable for inclusion in competitive routines.)

(For a slow movement on stage, swing your legs wide apart. Do a split if you're limber enough—and delay your pushaway. For a fast movement in a strictly tumbling routine, swing your legs closer together and push away as you pass the vertical upside-down position.

Come out of your handstand as if to walk backwards through or by means of a backward walkover.

Arch backward, feet approximately a short walking stride apart. Throw your hands backward to the mat while you kick vigorously upward with your free leg.

(Repeat in series, gaining distance in approximately walking strides. As you develop speed, try for enough lift from your kicks to get over, touching fingertips only lightly. Continue as you develop one-arm backward walkover handsprings and, later, a kickback somersault.)

KICKBACK
SOMERSAULT

Take off standing or from any preceding stunt which finishes in a forward lean with backward momentum.

Spring hand from your take-off leg as your free leg kick carries you into a backward lean.

Kick for maximum range up and back with your free leg. Throw your arms upward.

Make your follow-up kick with your take-off foot a continuation of your spring. Make your spring flow into your kick to increase its momentum.

Arch, look up, and throw your arms upward as you pass the vertical, upside-down position.

Try to land in a forward lean with continued backward circular momentum.

(Place your follow-up foot a short walking stride back of your landing foot to continue into a backward walkover, or place your feet even to complete a routine.)

CHAPTER FIVE

LESSON PLANS

(Because Steps I and II as recommended for the pike sequence also prepare for hand springs and related somersaults, we shall skip over to the next level of difficulty which involves a variation.)

Step III

The press-up to a head or hand balance from the preceding chapter features a steady pull by the muscles of the back and buttocks in lifting the legs from a pike position into an arch. Hand springs continue the leg swing, but a controlled recovery from an arch (a semi- or complete back bend position) becomes equally important. An opposite exercise to balance the knees-straight (pike) press-up is also needed. This is the back bend and recovery. A controlled back bend is also a useful stage or field stunt.

First, ask a companion (standing behind you and grasping your upraised hands) to lower you into a high reverse bridge, resting your weight on your head and feet only. Pull yourself up into an erect position with as little help from your companion as possible. Day by day pull harder to lift yourself out of the arch without using your hands and arms, as you depend less and less on your companion. When you can recover without assistance, begin to practice the bend backward. At first your companion may furnish support back of your neck as needed. Gradually diminish this support until you can easily do the back bend and recover.

Try for a relaxed kick-up to a hand balance. Learn to relax the muscles you're not using at a given instant. A tricky learning assist is to set a certain total time for holding handstands each work-out period. Ask a companion to time you with a stop watch if that is convenient. Counting every full second accomplished, repeat until a total of 30 seconds is accomplished, then 1 minute. Later count only each balance held for 5 seconds or better, then 10, then 15, and so on until a good balance is an established accomplishment.

Step IV

Practice dives into Arabian hand springs, as well as a series of Arabian hand springs. This is a surprising variation of a dive finish.

Step V

Girls, perfect your series of frontovers, backovers, and walkovers. Some boys can do series of fast walkovers.

Chapter 6
FROM BACK ROLL EXTENSION
TO BACKWARD LAYOUT

To the novice tumbler, the accomplishment of a single, good backward handspring is an occasion to celebrate. And it should be. A backward handspring is evidence of outstanding agility, co-ordination, and physical condition. When the young tumbler does his first backward hand spring he is *on his way.*

But an over-all view of tumbling places flipflaps (backward hand springs) as, chiefly, a means of building up backward momentum to convert to height in a more sensational stunt at the climax of a routine.

The young tumbler should practice repeatedly long series of flipflaps, trying for speed and more speed. He should keep in mind that he is working up to a climax and that the momentum of one preliminary stunt must flow smoothly into the next to *build up* for a climactic transition to height.

To gain speed, keep your flipflaps low. A beginning flipflap of a series is anything but a high backward dive. But as you gain speed, the upward hip thrust after the sit and the throw backwards lose emphasis to merge into a smooth, coasting arch backward. At this stage, your flipflaps may resemble a series of upside-down swan dives *through* (not hesitating in) hand springs.

When you have learned to exploit flipflaps for momentum, try some for height until your hands barely touch. When they don't touch, you have a backward layout (somersaults in layout position). When you get the feel of a beginning layout as, simply, a high flipflap, try for greater and greater height. Arch and extend your arms sideward and back for a swan layout as your body approximately parallels the mat (above it) and until you manipulate your arms for a balanced landing.

You don't have to do much after your take-off to make your body revolve during a flipflap or backward layout. Your arch places your body in the shape of a bow. If you flip a bow upward by applying force to one end, it will spin in the direction to which it is off balance. For the same reason, when you take off into an arched backward hand spring or somersault, your body will revolve. Your off-balance take-off throws your hips higher than your shoulders, and your throw-back causes your upper body to move backward and downward while your legs move upward. The result is stable, circular momentum as long as you hold your layout.

AN ADVANCED BACKWARD ROLL

Stand at attention, your back to the lane of mats.

Lean far forward and fall backward, knees stiff.

(Make your entry a complete jackknife, arms extended as illustrated, after you gain confidence. First, place your hands at your hips to cushion your fall.)

Sit, knees stiff. Increase your forward bend all the way into your landing. Touch your ankles for a complete pike as your hips strike the mat. Permit your weight to shift along your calves, thighs, and buttocks.

Rock back and flip your legs up. Execute your sit and rock so rapidly that no one bulge of muscle feels the shock of landing or carries your weight a perceptible interval of time.

Kick your legs straight up and snap your hips upward as high and as fast as possible.

Kip into a handstand. Permit your legs to fall back and place your hands back of your neck to assist your snap up.

Kip high to place your hips over your shoulders for a handstand.

Push off and snap down. A knee kick may dominate your snap down at first, but, as you become expert, a leg swing will add power.

Swing your legs under your hips. Throw your arms, shoulders, and head upward as a follow-through from your push-off into a spring for height.

Make your landing a spring for maximum height. (To be effective, your snapdown must convert to much greater height of spring than would be possible from a still crouch. A snapdown has no purpose other than as a reflex to build up momentum; concentrate so to establish it. Hundreds of purposeful repetitions may be necessary before snapdowns effectively accomplish their purpose.)

THE BACKWARD HANDSPRING
(in series, flipflaps)

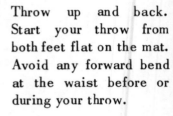

Check your balance.

Relax to a sitting position, your back straight. Permit your knees and hips to flex to 90° angles.

Throw up and back. Start your throw from both feet flat on the mat. Avoid any forward bend at the waist before or during your throw.

Thrust your hips vigorously up and forward as you arch backward. From feet flat, extend your ankles as for any other spring. Extend your knees and hips and arch your back simultaneously.

Reach for a firm hand contact. Relax your legs at this stage to permit a lightning shift to the snapdown reflex as your legs swing through the handstand position.

Permit circular momentum to whirl your legs through the handstand position. (Make your leg action a drive at your take-off; relaxed through the handstand; and a snap down past the handstand.)

Make your snapdown a continuation of the arc through which legs swing during your hand contact.

Push off and swing your legs down.

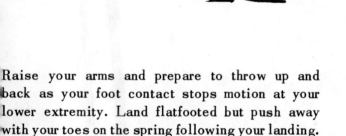

Raise your arms and prepare to throw up and back as your foot contact stops motion at your lower extremity. Land flatfooted but push away with your toes on the spring following your landing.

Throw and spring for height to dissipate momentum after a single spring or the completion of a series. (The reflex of an instantaneous follow-through from a backward hand spring, to gain either height or backward momentum, is vital to the building of routines. Never make a dead landing or kill momentum from a backward hand spring.)

THE BACKWARD SOMERSAULT
(layout)

Throw and spring high from the snapdown of a flipflap. Permit circular momentum to continue, as for another flipflap, your feet contacting the mat until your hips are slightly off balance in the direction of backward movement. Execute your hip thrust for a high rather than a low body spin.

Hold your layout arch through a complete backward revolution. You can coast in from here. Continued circular movement is due to the hip thrust of your take-off, and your altitude depends upon the unchecked speed of your preceding flipflap as converted to height. The precise backward-lean angle and range of leg extension (take-off spring) most effective must be established by consistent practice.

Land erect; knees only slightly bent. (From this landing you may snap into a quick forward tuck for a forward somersault or throw with your upper body for continued circular movement and another backward stunt.)

FLIPFLAPS AND BACKWARD LAYOUTS: LEARNING ASSISTS

For most people, the backward hand spring is more difficult than the back flip (a tucked backward somersault). This may be confusing to the learner because many coaches and writers insist that the backward hand-spring be mastered first.

It is true that if the tuck reflex dominated the arch reflex on an attempted flipflap, a bad fall might result. On the other hand, it is disconcerting to postpone an easier stunt which is a great deal of fun because, theoretically, a more difficult stunt should be learned first.

The solution is a clear distinction between the tuck and layout reflexes, both in understanding and experience. The flipflap may be literally learned in sections. There is no reason why a tuck reflex should interfere with the combination of these layout reflexes.

If you can head spring and kip to fully erect, arched landings, you have satisfactorily mastered the *abrupt arch* reflex, which emphasizes the hip thrust forward as the apex of the layout arch movement. True, you're going in the opposite direction on a flipflap, but that is incidental in so far as the hip thrust reflex is concerned. If your kip and head-spring arches will pick you up to layout arch landings, you're ready for the hip thrust into the arch of the flipflap. If not, a belt or spotter won't help much; both you and your partners are more or less wasting your time.

A second check on readiness for flipflaps is the ability to do repeated back bends and recoveries with reasonable comfort. There are two factors involved: a sufficiently limber back and a feeling of security in placing your hands on the mat back of your head.

This feeling of security also involves assurance that your hands, once placed, will support your weight through a fast handstand and push-off for the snapdown. The back roll extension (advanced back roll) is made to order to establish this assurance. If you can push into a hand-stand from a back roll, you can certainly support yourself through a handstand for which you already have sufficient height. It will require hundreds of these advanced back rolls to establish the handstand reflex of the flipflap; however, because they are a lot of fun and are extremely impressive in elementary routines, efforts to perfect them are very much worth while.

A third check is the ability to get a real bounce out of a snapdown. This, too, is part of the advanced back roll as illustrated. You should be able to raise your head at least 50 per cent higher from this snapdown bounce than from a standing spring, and as high as you can from a running spring upward. The hundreds of repetitions mentioned will do the job.

With these four reflexes firmly grounded (the snap arch into a layout position, the limber back bend, the hand placement through a fast handstand, and the snapdown into a high bounce) you're ready to put them together to make one flipflap. To give you confidence, a spotter or belt will help a great deal at this point, but you shouldn't need either of them very long.

Next, combine flipflaps into series. Make sure of smooth flowing rhythm through two, then three, four, five, and at least six if you have the mat space. When you have complete confidence, learn to perform as well across a big lawn. From this exercise go on to a flipflap-back flip. You have now three possible approaches to the backward layout: (1) Gradually increase the height of a final flipflap of a series until you don't touch your hands, then gradually assume the full layout position throughout the stunt; (2) work on flipflap-back flips and gradually open up from a tuck to a layout over a period of several weeks' practice; or, (3) with two assistants holding ropes to a belt around your waist, go into flipflap layouts until you have the confidence to try it with a lone spotter; then let your spotter step away while you work for height and more height and better form.

To spot a flipflap, press upward against the upper buttocks. The most frequent weakness to correct is a lack of power in the hip thrust. This thrust should be carried to an exaggerated height at first, then relaxed as assurance is gained.

Manipulate the safety belt to assure adequate height on the landing of a beginning layout.

Chapter 7
CARTWHEELS AND
SIDEWARD SOMERSAULTS

Cartwheels constitute a beautifully artistic manner of getting from one location on stage to another. Don't simply walk to get into position for your next stage routine: tumble to where you are supposed to be next. The sideward motion of a series of cartwheels blends smoothly with, and does not detract from, other action in progress.

A sideward somersault following a cartwheel or series of cartwheels is a climactic competitive stunt and one which is not overdone. Its novelty as well as difficulty may be counted upon to impress both judges and spectators.

The butterfly is primarily a girl's stunt. The stunt of its circular movement lends itself well to performance of series in a large circle on a stage or field. The action is violent and exotic and compels attention. Because it does not lend itself well to strictly lengthwise progress down a long mat, it belongs in the field of acrobatic dancing rather than of competitive gymnastics.

This chapter introduces the technique of creating circular momentum by means of a sideward rather than a backward arch and a sideward and upward rather than a backward and upward leg swing. The sideward arch is more than a simple sideward bend, because the outwardly braced leg—below the torso in the normally vertical position—forms part of the line of the sideward arch. The tumbler must now think in terms of the esthetic values of the line and form of two simultaneous arches: the sideward and the normal handstand.

Cartwheels are successions of alternating sideward arches while the line of the handstand arch is maintained throughout. The first arch is formed by lowering one shoulder and reaching for the mat with the corresponding hand, the second by lowering the opposite hip sideward (from the hips-above-head stage of the handstand) and swinging the leg downward. Each arch is a *throw* from an arch into an arch. As the action speeds up, the swing from an arch to one side into an arch to the opposite side becomes a *whip*. The hips are *whipped* up and over each time the hands contact the mat.

From a fast cartwheel you have the circular momentum needed for a sideward somersault. There are two possible techniques for getting the necessary height: a whip to lift the hips so high that the hand contact is not necessary for support, and a leg spring to convert sideward to upward momentum.

61

THE CARTWHEEL

Build up momentum by a slight run and make a 90° turn facing your judges or audience. Make your turn smoothly and freely and without losing speed.

Convert circular to momentum by a radical sideward bend and a sideward and upward swing with the opposite leg.

Swing your take-off leg in a follow-up action to go into the handstand.

Spin through a widespread handstand. Arch and hold your head up, toes pointed, in true, handstand form.

Land on your lead foot (as of your initial leg swing) in a sideward arch towards your take-off. Maintain continuous sideward motion as you whip over into an arch to your opposite side, landing—feet fairly wide apart—on your take-off leg. With no hesitation continue into succeeding revolutions.

THE BUTTERFLY

Face your audience, feet about 18 inches apart. Swing low to your right, bending your right knee.

As a recoil, swing your arms up and over as you twist violently to your left and very low.

Straighten your left knee, pushing hard with your left foot as you kick your right leg out and up.

Follow through with your body riding in a twist low and to your left until your left leg follows your right in an overhead whirl.

Land on your right foot, your head very near your right ankle and your left arm below your head.

Continue your slanting whirl by whipping around to your left (your original take-off) foot, your left knee bent as of your take-off.

Repeat for as many revolutions as are necessary to complete a circle or to cover the stage area at your disposal.

THE SIDEWARD SOMERSAULT
(with tuck)

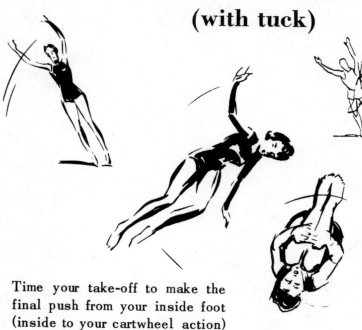

Take off from a cartwheel preceded by a short run.

Bring your feet closer together and make your take-off spring almost simultaneously from both feet.

Time your take-off to make the final push from your inside foot (inside to your cartwheel action) while you are off balance in that direction.

Pull your legs up into your tuck instantly.

Kick out of your tuck and straighten your body so as to make your landing position identical to that of your take-off.

THE SIDEWARD SOMERSAULT
(layout)

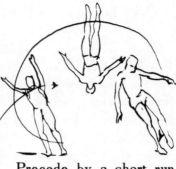

Begin your revolution by means of a simultaneous push from your left foot, while your body is over-balanced to your left, and a body whip sidewards.

Precede by a short run and a fast cartwheel.

Bring your feet closer together, knees slightly bent. Spring from both feet, but emphasize your final push from your left.

Practice to accomplish your evolution by as slight an obvious effort as possible. Skill developed by very many repetitions will enable you to accomplish your somersault with a short range of sharp muscular contraction and and scarcely noticeable effort.)

Keep your legs together, toes pointed, through three-fourths of your revolution. Make an erect, balanced landing, your body alignment the same as for your take-off.

For movement to your right, reverse your foot and torso action.)

CARTWHEELS AND SIDEWARD
SOMERSAULTS: LEARNING ASSISTS

From observing his own pupils do the cartwheel, the author would rate it as being moderately difficult. By means of a reach and a bend forward, beginners are able to do series of pseudo-cartwheels by going through the motions of merely alternating hand and foot contacts with the mat. Cartwheels are rather easy to do badly, whereas perfection is achieved neither easily nor very early in a tumbling experience.

Two techniques are essentially involved: manipulation of a handstand in any form, with hands and feet wide apart as arms and legs form a wide V, or any variation between this extreme form and a normal handstand—and creation and control of sideward momentum.

The handstand arch and the knees-straight, toes-pointed form should become a fixed reflex, and should follow through the complex revolution of every good cartwheel. The companion reflex vital to an excellent cartwheel is that of a body whip from a sideward arch to one side into a sideward arch to the other side.

Because of the danger of sloppy performance of cartwheels, novice tumblers are advised to work from the handstand as a base of operation. Achieve reasonable certainty of a kick up into a good handstand first, then whip into a handstand sideward. During the same exercise period, kick up into a normal handstand and whip out of it sideward. When both a whip into and out of a handstand are fairly easy, whip in *and* out. Swing sidewise into a handstand, hold, and swing sidewise outward to a standing position. Repeat, gradually swinging legs and arms further apart and speed up the swing until there is no stop in the handstand. That is one cartwheel; repeat and you have two. Continue until as many as you have space for are in good form.

When good form in fast cartwheels is established, begin to convert sideward to upward momentum from a cartwheel landing. Draw the legs closer together on the landing preceding an upward spring, speeding up the swing of the follow-up leg so that both feet land almost together. An accent on the take-off of the inside leg (inside to the circle to be prescribed by the somersault) will add impetus to circular momentum needed for the somersault.

For a layout sideward somersault, the upward whip of the hips must lift the body, complementing the effect of the spring from both legs.

Chapter 8
FROM ROUNDOFF TO FULL
TWISTING BACKWARD SOMERSAULT

The most spectacular recent advances in tumbling have been in the number of twists in backward somersaults. A few years ago a full twisting layout was a sensation. Currently, two and one-half twisting layouts are expected in national meets, and one wonders what is to come next.

How is such momentum, backwards, physically possible? Every youth center junior tumbler knows the answer. One cannot run backwards very fast. But he can run forward and a roundoff will readily convert forward speed to backward.

Stunts described in this chapter serve two purposes: to change the direction of momentum; and to constitute routine climaxes of amazing complexity and difficulty as made possible by a shift from forward to backward momentum. Reconversion from backward to forward by means of a half twisting backward somersault is also readily accomplished, and serves to lengthen a routine by two changes of direction during its progress.

The roundoff is the key to the multiple twisting somersaults, because it gets a flipflap off to a faster start and a still faster finish than would otherwise be possible. The roundoff may begin the build-up of backward momentum for a double backward somersault (in tuck position). Showier and more difficult than a roundoff but not quite so effective as a carry-over of momentum, the baroni serves the same purpose. It is a variety stunt to substitute occasionally for a roundoff in routines. On the trampoline, the baroni *must* replace the roundoff. The *whip* of the baroni, repeatedly performed over the trampoline, is excellent practice for the torso action of both the roundoff and the baroni on the mat, because not nearly so many practice repetitions would be possible during a workout on the mat. But go from the mat to the trampoline, not vice versa; let the trampoline practice carry over to the mat the next day.

The full and multiple twisting backward somersaults appear tremendously complex. Actually, what the tumbler does to set in motion this bewildering activity (to spectators) is comparatively simple. It is not that he does many things, but that his skill, through long practice, is such that his body responds so effectively to what he does do that non-expert observers are left without a satisfactory explanation of how he accomplishes a spin around a lengthwise, central head-to-foot axis.

THE ROUNDOFF

Run, skip on your right foot, and begin your throw from a forward lean over your left leg.

Swing your right leg upward and sideward and spring from your left foot.

Whip your hips and legs through a handstand by rotating your wrists, arms, and shoulders while you pull with the twisting muscles of your torso. Complete your half-twist in the handstand position.

Snap your legs down under your hips by a strong pull with your thigh and abdominal muscles. Push off with both hands.

Land in position for a powerful throw upward and back. Spring and throw into your following backward somersault or flipflap.

(Merge your landing on the roundoff with your spring and throw into your following stunt. Land with your knees slightly bent in order that your landing may *pass on* into your succeeding take-off all the momentum gained, absorbing none of it.)

HAND, WRIST, AND ARM ACTION
OF THE ROUNDOFF

Rotate your left arm and wrist to place your left hand on the mat, fingers spread and pointing at a sideward and backward angle.

Rotate your right arm and wrist in a similar manner and cross your right over your left.

Place your right hand close to your left and a little forward.

Plant your hands solidly and push and twist by means of wrist, arm, and shoulder rotation. To begin your *whip,* twist literally from your finger tips.

Push off vigorously to add momentum to your snapdown.

Bring your arms straight up and back from your roundoff landing to effect a smooth, powerful throw into a succeeding stunt.

THE BARONI

Run, as for a roundoff.

Swing your right leg powerfully upward as you drive hard from your left foot. Pull your left elbow backward and hook your raised right arm downward as you take off.

Throw your upper body forward (from the waist) and sideward. Twist your torso to the left, dropping your left shoulder.

Whip your body out of your left sideward bend by flexing the extended muscles of the right side of your torso. Don't drop your shoulders after you take off; whip your hips above your shoulders to straighten your body into an approximate layout.

Fling your head and shoulders to the left to guide your half-twist. Manipulate your legs also to motivate a fast twist and to get into position for a straight snapdown.

Complete your twist in the upside-down position.

Follow through (from the whip that straightens your body) into a snapdown. Make the snapdown part of the whip. Because speed for a fast, snappy landing is the essence of this stunt and the roundoff, make the whole movement a fast, twisting whip.

Extend your arms sideward to check your twist.

Pull your legs under your hips for a straight landing. Bring your arms into position for a throwback. into a succeeding stunt.

Land on balance for an instantaneous take-off into a backward somersault or flipflap.

HALF TWISTING BACKWARD SOMERSAULT

Snap down from a flipflap, roundoff, or baroni.

Throw up and back as for a back layout.

Motivate your twist by an arm hook across your chest and a shoulder thrust backwards.

Pull your arms in close to your chest to speed up your twist.

(Your twisting layouts must be very high in order to give an impression of good form and to provide time to manipulate the twists. Backward momentum preceding a throw and spring must, therefore, be very great as a result of fast movement backwards. You may build up this momentum by a series of flipflaps, roundoff and flipflaps, or a run into a baroni. A forward hand spring or tinsica will provide forward momentum which may be converted to backward by a roundoff or baroni. Work out your own individual routines to build up backward momentum.)

Accomplish your half twist in your reversed vertical position.

Raise and spread your arms in order to check your twist.

Hold or renew your arch as you fall, facing opposite to your take-off.

Look up and swing your legs under your hips for an erect landing.

Make a high, true layout landing. From this arm position you may take off into a forward somersault or hand spring.

(You must do five things to accomplish a good twisting layout: [1] Build up great backward momentum; [2] throw and spring for maximum height; [3] rotate your head sharply sideward, hook one arm across your chest and thrust the opposite shoulder backwards to begin your twist; [4] bring your arms in close to speed up your twist; and [5] land in a position to take off for a succeeding stunt.)

FULL TWISTING BACKWARD
SOMERSAULT

Snap down from a fast roundoff or flip-flap. Throw and spring upward for maximum height.

Fling your head to your right to look over your right shoulder. Hook your left arm to your right shoulder and thrust your left shoulder backwards.

Accomplish your half turn at your horizontal layout position. (At this stage, two movements are taking place: Your body is spinning to the right while it prescribes a circle around your upper chest as an axis.)

Draw your arms in close to your body to utilize centrifugal force for a fast spin. Accomplish your three-quarter turn in your reverse, vertical position.

(For a twist to the left simply substitute left for right and vice versa in the preceding text and formulate a mental image of the action as so described. The direction of the twist is optional as a matter of personal preference. Right or left sidedness is only one factor; another is whether the arm hook across the chest or the shoulder thrust backward is regarded as the stronger action in motivating the twist.)

Release your arm tension as your body passes through your reverse, vertical position.

Accomplish your full twist as your somersault is three-quarters completed. Raise and spread your arms to check your twist.

Look up as you fall into your take-off position.

Swing your legs under your hips for an erect landing to complete the 360° revolution of your somersault.

Land with a 14- to 15-inch foot spread for balance.

CHAPTER EIGHT
LEARNING EXPERIENCES

The arm and shoulder action responsible for a sideward twist should be established well in advance of the time when you are ready to combine it with the backward somersaults. It may be usefully employed in elementary and intermediate routines, but it must be understood first.

Stand erect, then dip and spring upward. At the peak of your spring, thrust your right shoulder backward abruptly and forcibly and see what happens. Your body easily prescribes a half twist. Try again, harder, and you'll make it a three-quarter twist. You might even execute a full twist very soon in this manner.

Now forget about your right shoulder movement and try something else. Spring, as before, but hook your left arm sharply across your chest to your right. Again you twist, and faster and further with less effort. Now put the two movements together and a full twist from a moderate spring will be easy. During the long ascent and equally long descent of a layout back somersault there will be time (approximately a full second) for from one to three turns. Nor is three necessarily the limit.

Put this reflex to work first as you perfect your bounce from the snapdown of the advanced back roll. Snap down from your handstand, then bounce and twist simultaneously. Work this into an elementary routine. For example, you could back roll into a handstand; snap down; bounce and twist fully and dive back towards your starting point; back roll again and snap down and twist; dive or spring in your original direction, in which you now face.

Half twisting snapdowns (twist after your push-away) may then be very effectively applied to the same type of routine. Half twisting forward and backward handsprings should eventually follow and may be usefully worked into routines. The twisting backward somersaults should follow naturally and without undue difficulty.

Chapter 9
A FINAL ROUNDUP OF STUNTS:
TINSICA, TIGNA, AND JONAH

Innumerable variations of basic stunts are possible. It does not necessarily follow that every movement which *can* be performed *should* be in competition or for exhibition. For example, a roundoff is an interesting movement, but not as beautiful as climactic stunts which it makes possible. Its purpose is to convert forward to backward momentum, so why weaken it by a one-hand contact? Likewise, the baroni is intended to change the direction of momentum; why do a Rudolph (a full twisting baroni) to defeat its purpose? Why remove one of the spokes of a cartwheel when you have only four to begin with?

No criticism of tumblers who specialize in novel variations is intended. The author merely suggests that every stunt should have a specific purpose in a routine, and that novelty of and for itself is more or less beside the point. The one-hand roundoff, the Rudolph, the one hand cartwheel, and numerous other *possible* variations are not illustrated in this book because they seem to have little or nothing to add to a routine.

Also, adaptations of basic stunts by acrobatic dancers are either suggested or omitted. Much of Chapter Five deals with the area of overlap between acrobatic dancing and tumbling. Simple adaptations of basic stunts to both stage and straight-line routine tumbling are illustrated. It is impractical to include involved theatrical acrobatics in this book, but recognition of elementary theatrical terminology is necessary to avoid confusion.

Theatrical adaptations are neither more beautiful nor more difficult than climactic stunts featured in this book; they differ because a stage differs from a long narrow mat in shape and because trick lighting and catchy music is part of the theater, while a gymnasium is flatly lighted for a clear view (no tricks) and the only music is the cheering of partisan spectators or free or businesslike conversation. The butterfly (Chapter Six) belongs primarily to the stage whereas cartwheels and hand springs (Chapter Five) may be adapted for either stage or mat. Our overlap is limited to these variations, which are included partly to aid in the staging of field events (for example, football half-time entertainments), because an athletic field may be both theater and gymnasium.

THE TINSICA

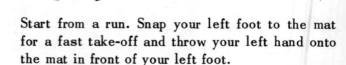

Start from a run. Snap your left foot to the mat for a fast take-off and throw your left hand onto the mat in front of your left foot.

Swing your right leg backward and upward simultaneously with the spring from your left foot. Place your right hand 12 to 18 inches in front of your left as part of your initial throw for a two-hand placement.

Execute an energetic arch spring to carry your hands off the mat before your right foot lands. Bring your right foot to the mat close to the take-off point of the right hand, 20 to 30 inches in front of your left foot.

Push off with your right hand.

(To slow down forward momentum, place your left foot well in advance of your right. To speed up forward movement, or to follow with a tigna, bring your left foot down fast, close to and instantly following your right foot contact. Throw your left arm straight overhead and land with your knees slightly bent in order to take off from both feet for a tigna.)

THE TIGNA

Lift your shoulders as high as possible on your tinsica landing.

Use the momentum of the tinsica to carry you into a tucked forward somersault.

Permit your right shoulder to drop naturally, following through the action and arm-position of the tinsica landing.

Force your left shoulder as high as possible for a sideward effect. Exploit your high shoulder position to effect a very fast lunge into a tuck.

Kick out of your tuck so as to land your right foot slightly before your left. (Place your left conveniently in front of your right foot for a take-off into another tinsica. Go into another tinsica or a tigna without the slightest hesitation. Make every move blend with the one to follow so that spectators are impressed with your series as a single, flowing movement. On the final tigna of a series, kick out of your tuck fast and land erect with your feet together. Tinsica-tigna combinations in swingtime emphasize finesse, a mastery of the ultimate in tumbling rhythm.)

79

THE JONAH

Run to build up maximum speed, shorten your final stride, and bring your feet together. Take off for a long, high dive.

Leap into a high swan. Make your arch and arm action sharp and showy, and time your perfect swan for the peak of your ascent.

Twist your torso to your left, dropping your right shoulder, and bend downward from your waist. Make your twist and bend one motion, sharp and clear-cut; don't rotate your hips or bend your knees sharply at this stage. Co-operate with gravity; make your bend, for your center of gravity would fall anyway. This permits you to raise your hips still higher as you pull into your tuck.

Tuck, pulling your legs up against your chest. Thrust your left shoulder backwards and slap your knee against your left breast. Grasp your right shin with your right hand and pull as for a normal tuck.

Tuck tight to speed up the spin resulting from your arm and leg action.

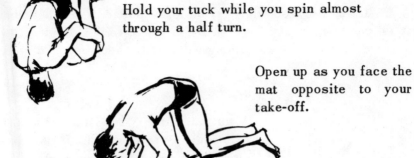

Hold your tuck while you spin almost through a half turn.

Open up as you face the mat opposite to your take-off.

Swing your legs under your hips and look up as for a normal somersault.

Straighten out as completely as possible for a balanced landing.

(A Jonah is ordinarily a one-stunt routine. It is spectacular enough to stimulate your audience and its extraordinary difficulty may be counted upon to impress your judges. When you're good enough, try this for either the opener or the climax of a four-routine performance.)

Chapter 10
BASIC EXERCISES

Leading up to the Cradle

A cradle is comparatively easy on a trampoline, and is a beautiful stunt. It is even more impressive on the mat but very difficult. The following exercises, of excellent training value in themselves, lead up to a cradle.

Step I

A roll back into a headstand is elementary, but will probably require considerable practice over a period of several weeks. Work at it until it becomes a fixed reflex.

A very pleasing stage routine and further development of your kip will result from the following combination: Begin with a pike style press-up to a headstand. Let back down until your toes brush the mat. Headspring to erect stance without a leg push.

Step II

Stopping a back roll extension in the handstand is of secondary difficulty and probably will not follow Step I immediately. Work at it and have patience. This, too, will become reflex action and may be used as a stage routine.

The Cradle

Spring back as for a flipflap, check your progress in the handstand, let down to the back of your neck immediately, and kip. Work up to four to eight repetitions.

Mule Kicks

This is a rugged exercise to establish the snapdown reflex. Spring up into a handstand, legs together, and snap down. Repeat.

For a mule kick, spring instantly and vigorously from your snapdown landing, whipping your legs back and up as you swing your arms forward into an instantaneous handstand; push off, snap down and repeat. Work up to six or eight smooth repetitions.

Twisting Snap Downs

First, do a back roll extension into a handstand, snap down with a half twist. As you push off, fling your head to your right and up, uppercut with your left hand across your chest, and thrust your right shoulder hard backward. Establish a good landing facing opposite to your stance at the beginning of your backward roll. Repeat four to six times.

Half Twisting Flipflap

A half twisting flipflap is an easy step from the foregoing exercise. Repeat four to six times. Continue over a period of several weeks until you are sure of a half twisting snapdown wherever you may want it.

Chapter 11
BUILDING ROUTINES

Variety and a change of pace attract and hold attention. You may fascinate by sheer beauty of rhythmic movement, surprise with a change of tempo or direction or both, and thrill by a spectacular climax. Build all these elements, carefully placed, into your routines.

One of a group of routines may be entirely rhythmic. Swingtime performance prevents judges or spectators from visualizing your routine as separate stunts. Probably the simplest example of such a routine is a series of high-arching, pike-type head springs with a layout finish.

A series of flipflaps in the same form and, perhaps with the same finish, is of moderate difficulty.

Three tinsica-tigna combinations constitute a routine of extreme difficulty and amazing complexity in fast, continuous action.

A change of direction, effectively accented, is always surprising. In an elementary routine, the following (back roll extension, chest roll, snap through, back roll extension) is surprising and pleasing.

You may go into this from either backward or forward movement and proceed from it either way, into a back flip or forward somersault, dive, or forward spring.

A spectacular one-event routine, ranging in difficulty from a long, high dive through a high forward somersault or a pike full, to a Jonah or double forward somersault, is instantaneously arresting. Almost to a person, your audience will draw a deep breath and hold it until you have recovered from your landing.

The third type of routine involves a build-up to a spectacular finish. Your audience senses that what you do first is simply preparation, and tension mounts as you approach your climax.

The art of building up to a climax requires long and careful practice. Begin as soon as you can do a good backward somersault. Simply go into your somersault from the bounce from the snapdown of a backroll extension finish.

Backward Progression No. 1

The merging of the momentum of the high bounce into the knee raise for the somersault is tricky. Your fastest upward motion will be precisely as your knees snap straight on the spring (toes leaving the mat). Your knee bend must begin instantaneously at that point and speed up until your thighs slap your chest.

Backward Progression No. 2

As soon as you master a flipflap, substitute it for the back flip after the back roll extension. Instead of a spring almost straight up as for the back flip, sit back on the snapdown landing and throw your hips upward into a strong, high arch *as* you straighten your knees. This will throw you into the handstand of the flipflap without a knee bend. Snap down to finish.

Backward Progression No. 3

Your third step in building for a backward progression climax is to carry the momentum of the snapdown from a flipflap into a back flip. There is more backward momentum from the snapdown of the flipflap than from the snapdown of the back roll extension because backward momentum is greater. This, converted into height by the spring upward during the body swing backward, makes the flip easier and higher.

Backward Progression No. 4

Substitute a roundoff for a back roll extension to lead into a flipflap. Follow with a back flip.

Backward Progression No. 5

Skip into a handspring, roundoff, flipflap, back flip.

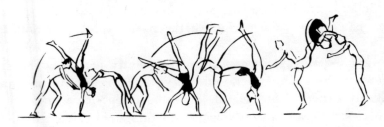

Backward Progression No. 6

Next, gradually open into a backward layout instead of a back flip. Finally, go into a half twisting layout which reverses your direction. Add stunts in this direction, reverse your direction a second time, and proceed on down to the end of the mat in your original direction. This constitutes a complex, difficult variety routine.

There are two natural climaxes after a build-up of ultimate backward momentum. The double backward somersault performed by a recent national champion was as follows: roundoff; flipflap; half twisting backward somersault; forward handspring; forward somersault; roundoff; flipflap; double backward somersault.

A build-up for a two and one-half twisting backward somersault was accomplished by the same tumbler as follows: roundoff; backward somersault; twisting flipflap; roundoff; flipflap; two and one-half twisting backward somersault.

The forward somersault after any twisting back full comes as a surprise and emphasizes the fact that the tumbler performed his climax with sufficient ease to follow with a pleasing anticlimax.

Unfortunately, the forward combinations have been rather neglected by American tumblers. Of course there is a reason: a double twisting back full is practical, something the expert may perfect in good form. Authorities disagree as to whether a true forward layout is possible in excellent form. A full twisting forward layout somersault, in the same form as that in which champions have performed the back layout somersault, seems remote.

Forward twisting somersaults are frequently performed on the stage as somewhere between a tuck and a layout. This form is not that which is ordinarily expected by current judges of competitive tumbling. Therefore these stunts are not illustrated in this book, because the author considers them to belong at present in the field of theatrical tumbling.

We should, however, work more seriously on the forward combinations, both in order to determine what is possible or practical and to try to match advanced backward progressions with comparable forward-moving routines.

Assuming you can go into a dive so as to utilize the momentum of the first dive to make the second smoother and easier, the next step may very well be a dive into a forward somersault. This presupposes a good, high, forward somersault with a tight tuck. This is very similar to your dive into a dive, with one exception: The dive-somersault combination demands an instantaneous flexion from the knee extension of the spring into a tight tuck.

Forward Progression No. 1

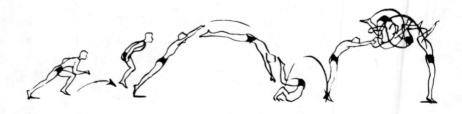

Forward Progression No. 2

A roll into a somersault is much more difficult but should be mastered by anyone who aspires to be an expert.

Forward Progression No. 3

After your roll-flip combination, learn a forward hand spring, forward somersault sequence.

Land with your arms high from the hand spring, and swing into a slight forward lean in order to convert forward momentum to height by a very fast leg extension from your hand spring. Leg flexion into your tuck must follow instantly.

Forward Progression No. 4

The momentum of a pike full will convert readily into a long, high dive, which will convert into a forward tucked somersault. It is easier to finish with a roll and looks better. Try this before friendly critics and see what they think of it.

Use your imagination. No combination of stunts is justified simply because it is possible. Plan your routines for pattern and effect.

CONCLUSION

Training Procedures and Attitudes

Continued repetitions of a stunt in poor form because that is the easy way to have fun and a faster approach to stunts of greater difficulty establishes poor form. But even the best coaching will not establish correct reflexes immediately, because there is not direct, conscious control over those greater areas of nervous activity which are unconscious. Continued practice, while aware of one's current limitations but making every effort to perfect one's form, will eventually establish correct reflexes. Practice the best form of which you are capable and trust your body to develop excellent form in due time.

Good form in every preliminary stunt is vitally important. Patience in perfecting elementary reflexes will save time in the long run. For example, if the toes-pointed legs-together style is a fixed reflex through forward and backward rolls, it will carry over into the somersaults. If you rush into the somersaults before this form is reflex action, you may never develop excellent form. Throughout Chapters Two to Seven of this book are step-by-step examples of reflex patterns of gradually increasing complexity.

Organizing a Workout

If you are a serious, determined athlete, the organization of a tumbling workout inevitably presents a dilemma. You need the strength and stamina developed by strenuous, continuous activity that leaves you dripping with perspiration. A solid hour of arduous, persistent repetition of difficult stunts three to five times a week will result in a peak of sheer physical power. But you also need supple muscles which will relax freely after every sharp tension and preparatory to every *super* effort. The arduous, persistent workout may leave you with too firm a prevailing muscle tone unless you establish a counter control.

Coaches and athletes differ in their methods of solving this problem. Some emphasize stretching and relaxing exercises before and during a workout period. Some work strenuously for short periods, consciously and systematically relaxing between supreme efforts and difficult stunts.

The young athlete is advised to study the matter of a muscle's relaxation in preparation for and after sharp tension, as seriously as the tension itself. The most effective muscular contraction is a sharp, instantaneous tension from a state of as complete a relaxation as is compatible with good posture. Especially, learn to relax before every supreme effort

90

in order that the crucial tension may be of the greatest possible impetus and power.

The following organization for serious tumbling practice seems to the author to be logical: (1) a warm-up period given to free and easy repetitions of elementary stunts which are still fun and which conform to correct form; (2) serious efforts to learn the difficult stunt which the tumbler has chosen to emphasize at a given time, or combinations of stunts; (3) stretching and relaxing exercises to develop power and stamina or multiple repetitions of stunts of moderate difficulty to reinforce correct reflexes; (4) a thorough but businesslike shower; and (5) a following activity (within 24 hours) of a particularly relaxing nature something comparatively light and free and not involving power as a primary factor.

The Tumbling Meet

A. A. U. contest rules specify that, for men, tumbling shall be limited to four routines of not over two minutes duration each. For women there is required one optional routine of not more than one and one-half minutes duration. Strictly tumbling routines must be performed; contortional or dance movements are not considered to be tumbling routines.

The mat is primarily a safety device. Participants may run onto the mat or leave it at the further end for the purpose of getting a running start for a backward trip. A brief rest period in conventional stance is permitted as one end of the mat is reached and again as the routine is completed. Tumbling on the floor on either side of the mat is penalized as poor form.

High school, collegiate, or community organization rules vary as appropriate authorities may determine.

A *referee* assumes general charge of a meet. A. A. U. rules specify five judges, one of whom is appointed to be head judge by the referee. Judges place themselves apart and on opposite sides of a competitor. Each judge, following an initial consultation after a beginning performance, scores on a basis of 10 for a perfect performance of extreme difficulty. Scorers record points awarded. Finesse is generally considered more important than difficulty.

GLOSSARY

ACROBATIC DANCING—Rhythmic tumbling routines performed on a stage as theatrical entertainment.

AERIAL—Any somersault, usually applied to acts of a theatrical nature rather than to competitive tumbling.

ARABIAN HAND SPRING—A hand spring with legs even or together throughout.

ARCH—Bending the body into a bow by thrusting the hips forward and bending the spinal column backward. Pointing the toes completes the "bow" effect in reverse balance or in the air.

ARCH DOWN—A chest roll downward from a hand balance.

ARCH OVER AND TWIST—A spring from the toes, head on the mat, into a reverse bridge, followed by a twist sideward, returning the body to a front bridge.

ARM HOOK—An abrupt and very fast arm flexion, elbow bent, to throw one arm across the chest at some degree of upward slant.

ARM SWING—A very fast arm raise, usually with elbows straight or only slightly bent.

BACK BEND—An arch backwards to rest the hands on the mat below the head.

BACK HAND SPRING, BACKWARD HAND SPRING (FLIPFLAP)—A spring from both feet into a backward arch and with a "whip" through the handstand position, completed by a snapdown.

BACKOVER—A slow backward hand spring, actually a back bend and recovery, permitting the legs to swing apart (one in advance) between take-off and landing but beginning and ending with legs together.

BACKWARD ROLL, BACK ROLL—A roll backward into a tuck and completing a 360° turn to a vertical stance.

BACKWARD ROLL EXTENSION—A backward roll, often with pike entry, with upward extension of the legs into a hand balance followed by a snapdown; a flange; advanced backward roll.

BACKWARD SOMERSAULT, BACK SOMERSAULT, BACK FLIP—A spring upward and a 360° turn backwards with no hand contact or other supporting assist; form may be layout, tuck, or a compromise typical of most whipover backward somersaults in series and of most girls' aerials.

BACKWARD TUCK—A tuck motivated by a forceful leg flexion, thighs drawn to the chest while the knees bend fully.

BARONI, BARANI, BORANI; BRANDY or BROWNY—A somersault with a body whip and a sideward twist to reverse the direction faced upon landing; a half twisting somersault converting forward to backward momentum; a roundoff without a hand spring.

BOUNDER FULL—One of a series of forward somersaults (swingtime) in some degree of compromise between tuck and layout form.

BRIDGE—The body supported by head and feet or head, hands and feet only, either in forward bend or backward arch position.

BUCK—A stunt in which the performer dives to his hands, pushes away, and snaps back to a forward-lean vertical stance on both feet.

BUCKING BRONCO—Rapidly repeated bucks.

BUTTERFLY—An aerial in the manner of a slanting cartwheel, usually a take-off from the left foot simultaneously with a sideward and downward left arm fling; done in series in a circle.

CARTWHEEL—A sideward hand spring, usually repeated in a series, keeping the arms and legs so spread as to create the illusion of spokes of a turning wheel.

CARTWHEEL HANDSTAND—A cartwheel finishing with a half turn and a pause in a hand balance position.

CARTWHEEL SOMERSAULT—A sideward somersault in cartwheel position; a cartwheel movement with sufficient "lift" to render a hand support unnecessary.

CHEST ROLL—A roll down from a handstand, body arched, landing on the chest and rolling backward along the abdomen and thighs until the toes touch.

CRADLE—A spring backwards to a shoulder balance followed by a neck spring; usually repeated swingtime.

CRADLE ROCK—A roll back to the shoulders after a neck spring and then repeated.

DEAD-LIFT JUMP — An upward or forward spring from a stationary crouch without benefit of momentum from a previous movement.

DEAD PRESS — Pull up from a prone to a pike position and press up into a head or hand balance.

DIVE — A spring upward and forward from both feet, breaking the subsequent fall with both hands and rolling through a tuck and up to a vertical stance or into a high bounce to dissipate the momentum gained; a forward roll after a spring, clearing the feet before the hand contact.

DIVING HAND SPRING — A dive onto the hands with a hand spring finish; usually but not necessarily an Arabian hand spring.

DOUBLE BACKWARD SOMERSAULT — Two 360° turns in the air by means of a tight forward tuck after a fast run; landing in a vertical squat.

DOUBLE TWISTING BACKWARD SOMERSAULT — A backward somersault in layout form while the body twists sideward through two 360° turns.

EXTENSION ROLL, ADVANCED BACKWARD ROLL, FLANGE — A backward roll to a momentary hand balance, followed by a snapdown.

FLANGE — An extension into a hand balance from a backward roll.

FLIPFLAP — A backward hand spring, usually one of a series or following a roundoff as a means of developing backward momentum.

FOLLOW THROUGH — Movement due to contraction of one group of muscles carried directly into continued movement powered by another group of muscles, resulting in greater freedom and range of movement and increased momentum.

FOREARM BALANCE — An inverted stand on the forearms, head clear of the mat.

FORWARD LAYOUT — A forward somersault while maintaining a body arch as opposed to a tuck, usually accomplished through part of the revolution, as in the pike full, or incompletely as in a girls' aerial.

FORWARD LEAN — Correct postural alignment while the body is slanted forward.

FORWARD ROLL — A roll forward in tucked position, finishing on both feet after a 360° revolution.

FORWARD TWISTING SOMERSAULT — A forward somersault with a sideward twist.

FROG HAND BALANCE — A press-up to a hand balance from a forward rest squat.

FROG-STYLE HEADSTAND — A press-up to a head and hand balance from a forward squat, thighs resting on upper arms just above the elbows.

FRONT BRIDGE — Body resting on head and toes and balls of the feet only, facing down to the mat; girls usually combine with a hand support assist.

FRONT HAND SPRING, FORWARD HAND SPRING — A forward running spring from both hands to both feet.

FRONT SOMERSAULT, FORWARD SOMERSAULT — A complete forward rotation in the air from feet take-off to feet landing.

FRONTOVER — A slow forward hand spring, usually in series, with an exaggerated arch; principally a girls' parade or theatrical technique.

FULL GAINER — A forward run, leap, and backward somersault while the body continues to move forward.

FULL TURN — A complete rotation of the body on its long axis.

FULL TWISTING BACKWARD SOMERSAULT — A backward somersault with a full twist, resulting in a landing facing as of the take-off.

GAINER — A backward somersault while the body is moving forward.

HALF TWISTING BACKWARD SOMERSAULT — A backward somersault during which the body twists sideward 180° to land facing opposite to the take-off position.

HAND BALANCE, HANDSTAND — Body in reverse, vertical stance, balanced over the hands, back arched to place the feet overhead with toes pointed. ("Hand balance" is the preferred academic term, but "handstand" is common gymnasium usage. The academic distinction seems to the author to be unimportant and likely to lose out in the long run.)

HAND SPRING — A spring, forward or backward, from hands to feet.

HEAD AND HAND BALANCE — The popular headstand as the author sees it, technically.

HEAD BALANCE — Body in reverse, vertical position, balanced on the head only; a professional acrobatic technique. ("Head balance," the usual academic designation for the popular "handstand," seems to leave no means of distinguishing the "professional" balance on the head only.)

HEAD SPRING — A spring from the head by means of a leg swing and a strong arch, take-off and landing on both feet, feet even.

HIGH DIVE — A dive for height, sacrificing lateral distance for altitude.

HIP EXTENSION — A hip thrust forward, forcing the body into an arch.

HIP THRUST — An abrupt hip extension, motivated by contraction of the large muscles of the buttocks and a backward arch.

JACKKNIFE — A position with the knees straight and toes pointed, the hips flexed.

JONAH — A high dive into a swan layout, followed by a forward and sideward tucked somersault.

JUMP THROUGH — From face down, body and arms extended, a jump through the extended arms to a sitting position.

KICKBACK SOMERSAULT — A backward somersault initiated by a kick forward and upward to place the kicking foot above and well back of the head as of the take-off with the opposite foot.

KICKOUT — A vigorous body extension out of a tuck in preparation for the landing after a somersault turn.

KICKOVER — A forward somersault motivated by a vigorous backward and upward kick with one leg and a spring take-off from the opposite leg.

KIP — From prone position on back, legs flexed at the hips, a leg swing and arch to project the body into a vertical landing on both feet.

LAYOUT — The position the body assumes when extended into an over-all arch, the direct opposite of a tuck.

LEAD-UP TRICK — A trick that is relatively simple but which leads to or contributes to the learning of more difficult stunts.

LEG DRIVE — A leg extension for the purpose of forcibly projecting the body forward or upward.

LEG SWING — A hip extension, thrusting one or both legs, straight or nearly so, forcibly backward through a wide range of movement. (In head down position the swing is, of course, to overhead and in advance of the head.)

LEOTARD — A tight, one-piece garment often worn by ballet dancers during training.

LUNGE — An abrupt and forceful forward reach, as for a tuck during a forward somersault.

MULE KICK — A forward dive into a hand balance followed instantaneously by a snapdown. Mule kicks are usually repeated as a fast exercise.

NECKSPRING — A roll forward into a kip.

NIP-UP — A neckspring.

NOVELTY — A stunt not listed as a standard maneuver.

ONE AND ONE-HALF FORWARD SOMERSAULT — A somersault continued into a dive landing.

ONE-HAND HANDSPRING — Any spring from one hand to one foot or both feet.

PIKE — A full forward bend at the waist, toes pointed and hands extended to the ankles if free from the mat.

PIKE FULL — A forward somersault motivated by a leg swing from a pike into a layout position.

PRESS — A method of getting into a head or hand balance by means of a steady pull as opposed to a kick-up.

REVERSE BRIDGE, WRESTLER'S BRIDGE — An upward hip thrust to form a body arch, head and feet or head, hands, and feet only touching the mat.

ROCK UP — A stunt in which the performer rolls, from a standing position, down to the knees, belly, chest, and hands, and then pushes up to a hand balance.

ROLL — To turn, head over heels, in a tucked position.

ROLL DOWN — To come down from a head or hand balance by lowering to the shoulders and executing a tucked roll forward.

ROUNDOFF — A forward hand spring with a half twist, hands so placed as to facilitate a body whip; a means of developing and converting forward to backward momentum.

ROUTINE — A series of stunts executed in a straight line down a considerable length of mat surface.

RUDOLPH — A full twisting baroni.

SHOULDER BALANCE — Legs extended upward, body resting on shoulders and reversed hand placement only.

SHOULDER ROLL — A sideward tucked roll.

SHOULDER SPRING — A neck spring.

SHOULDER THRUST — An abrupt and forceful shoulder extension backward; part of the mechanism of the sideward twist.

SIT BACKWARD — A backward fall to a sitting position of the mat, checking the fall with hands at the hips, fingers forward.

SIT THROUGH — A thrust of both legs through the extended arms of a forward-lean rest.

SNAPDOWN — A simultaneous push off and downward kick from a hand balance to a springy landing on the balls of the feet.

SNAP THROUGH — From front rest position (body extended, face down, weight on hands and toes) the legs are thrust between extended arms and through a sitting position to an extended reach forward, weight on hands and heels.

SNAP-UP — A neck spring.

SOMERSAULT — A complete turn in the air from feet to feet.

SPOT — To guard or assist the performer in order to prevent injury.

SPOTTER — Any trick executed in a small area; a take-off and landing in approximately the same spot.

SPRING — A revolution from feet to hands to feet.

SPRING-OVER — A spring from a front to a reverse bridge.

SQUAT — Lowering the body by means of a bend at the knees and hips.

SQUAT BALANCE — Frog-style balance, arms across thighs in a forward-lean balance over the hands.

SQUAT PRESS-UP — A press-up to a head or hand balance from a forward-lean squat balance over the hands.

SWINGTIME — Progress from one stunt into another so smoothly as to obscure the technical completion of one stunt and the beginning of another.

THROW — An abrupt and forceful bend forward or arch backward to begin a handspring or somersault.

TIGNA — A forward somersault from the landing of a tinsica.

TINSICA — A forward handspring with one foot and the corresponding hand in advance of the other.

TOE POINT — A full extension of the feet to improve form.

TRICK — Any gymnastic maneuver.

TUCK — A complete body flexion, curling the performer into a ball; the precise opposite of a body extension as a layout.

TWIST — A turn of the body on its long axis.

TWISTING FLIPFLAP — A sideward twist from the push-away of a backward handspring, causing the body to face opposite to the take-off position; may reverse the direction of progress in a routine.

TWO AND ONE-HALF TWISTING BACKWARD SOMERSAULT — A backward somersault in layout form while the body twists through two and one-half turns sideward, landing in a position opposite to that of the take-off.

UPSTART — A neck spring.

WALKOVER — A hand spring with legs spread as for a walking stride on take-off and landing.

WALKOVER SOMERSAULT — The preceding movement without a hand contact, as an aerial.

WHIP — A vigorous, powerful pullover to get sufficient force to execute a stunt so as to build up momentum.

WHIPBACK — A backward somersault with the same action as a backward handspring, usually done in a series, swingtime.

WRESTLER'S BRIDGE — A hip thrust upward, body resting on head and feet only.

INDEX